Xtreme Adventure

TREASURE HUNTING

BY S.L. HAMILTON

Visit us at
www.abdopublishing.com

Published by ABDO Publishing Company, PO Box 398166, Minneapolis, MN 55439.
Copyright ©2014 by Abdo Consulting Group, Inc. International copyrights reserved in all countries. No part of this book may be reproduced in any form without written permission from the publisher. A&D Xtreme™ is a trademark and logo of ABDO Publishing Company.

Printed in the United States of America, North Mankato, Minnesota.
102013
012014

 PRINTED ON RECYCLED PAPER

Editor: John Hamilton
Graphic Design: Sue Hamilton
Cover Design: Sue Hamilton
Cover Photo: Alamy
Interior Photos: AP-pgs 6-7, 12-13, 14, 15, 16 (inset), 20, 21, 23, 24, 25, 26 & 32; Corbis-pg 19 (top); Getty Images-pgs 8-9, 10-11, 18, 28 & 30-31; National Geographic-pgs 22 & 27; Science Source-pgs 4-5 & 19 (bottom); Thinkstock-pgs 1, 2-3, 16-17 & 29.

ABDO Booklinks
Web sites about Xtreme Adventure are featured on our Book Links pages. These links are routinely monitored and updated to provide the most current information available.
Web site: www.abdopublishing.com

Library of Congress Control Number: 2013946165

Cataloging-in-Publication Data

Hamilton, S.L.
 Treasure hunting / S.L. Hamilton.
  p. cm. -- (Xtreme adventure)
Includes index.
ISBN 978-1-62403-215-8
1. Treasure troves--Juvenile literature.   I. Title.
622/.19--dc23

2013946165

CONTENTS

TREASURE HUNTING

Treasure hunters search underwater and on land. They look for such treasure as gold, silver, jewelry, and even historical artifacts.

Some treasure hunters spend many hours researching old maps, diaries, letters, newspapers, and disaster reports for clues. Others simply go out looking for treasure using modern equipment, such as metal detectors. A lucky few find riches, but all find adventure.

XTREME FACT – The most valuable treasure hunter's find was the wreck of the Spanish galleon Nuestra Señora de Atocha in 1985. The treasure is valued at more than $450 million.

TOOLS & EQUIPMENT

A treasure hunter's most useful tool is a metal detector with headphones. There are metal detectors made for use on land and some for underwater. The detector sends an audio signal to the searcher. Many of today's detectors also have a visual display that points to what may be buried.

XTREME FACT – Treasure hunters spend a lot of time walking. Good shoes, a handheld GPS device, extra batteries, and water are important items to carry.

Some metal detectors are very sensitive and expensive, while others are cheap and lightweight. Some can be programmed to find specific things such as gold or silver.

Underwater treasure hunters require scuba gear and diving knowledge. Some treasure hunters use a device called a "mailbox blower." Treasure hunter Mel Fisher came up with the idea when he wanted the ocean's clear water near the surface to be blown down to the often murky bottom. Clear water would help divers see better. The blower also blew away centuries of accumulated sand, sometimes uncovering important artifacts and clues.

XTREME FACT – Blowers have caused 20-to-30-foot (6-to-9-m)-wide and 2-to-3-foot (.6-to-.9-m)-deep holes in the ocean bottom. Some people say this destroys part of the ocean floor.

DANGERS

Some treasure hunters travel deep into forests or walk to remote beaches and shorelines. Getting lost or hurt is possible. A GPS unit, cell or satellite phone, and a hiker's first-aid kit should be carried by treasure hunters.

XTREME FACT – Treasure hunters should always let a friend, family member, or local law enforcement official know where they are planning to walk or dive.

Underwater treasure hunters must be skilled divers. There is a risk of drowning in wrecks or from diving equipment malfunctions. Always dive with a partner.

HUNTING FOR COINS

Coins may be made of gold, silver, bronze, nickel, or copper. Millions of them have been created, carried, used, and lost. Because there have been so many coins made, they are easy to find.

Dr. Dieter Noli counts gold coins that were found near the coast of Namibia, Africa.

Coin hunters are often seen searching parks, beaches, and old shipwrecks. Some coins are not worth more than their face value, but finding them is still a fun adventure. However, every coin hunter searches for the "big find." These are coins that are rare, old, or unusual. Coins that were hammered or milled are valuable finds. Cast coins with a mistake on them, or ones in which only a limited number were produced, are also treasured finds.

XTREME FACT– People who look for old coins are called "coin shooters."

Archaeologist Alan Graham excavates the Frome hoard from a field in England.

In April 2010, treasure hunter Dave Crisp found a hoard (collection) of coins in a clay pot buried in a field near the town of Frome, England. Rather than dig it up himself, Crisp reburied it and alerted archaeologists.

The Frome hoard turned out to be 52,503 silver and bronze Roman coins from the 3rd century AD. It became the largest collection of coins ever found in Great Britain.

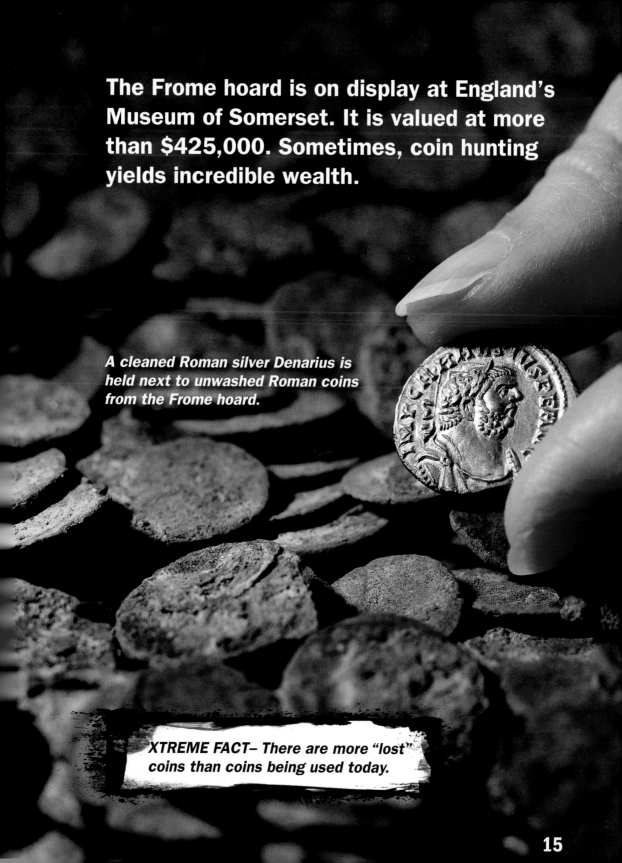

The Frome hoard is on display at England's Museum of Somerset. It is valued at more than $425,000. Sometimes, coin hunting yields incredible wealth.

A cleaned Roman silver Denarius is held next to unwashed Roman coins from the Frome hoard.

XTREME FACT– There are more "lost" coins than coins being used today.

HUNTING FOR JEWELRY

Beaches are popular jewelry hunting locations. People lose, misplace, and drop precious jewelry. Sunscreen makes hands slippery. Water makes skin shrink. People take off their jewelry and leave it on their towel, only to forget it and shake it out in the sand. Beach treasure hunters with metal detectors have found diamond rings and bracelets, gold class rings and watches, pearl earrings and pins, and emerald necklaces.

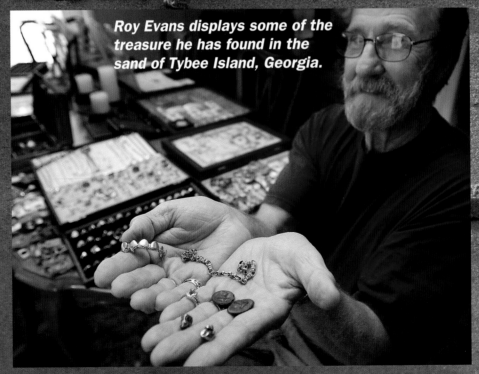

Roy Evans displays some of the treasure he has found in the sand of Tybee Island, Georgia.

XTREME FACT – Some treasure hunters not only find expensive jewelry, but many go on a hunt to find the original owner. Sometimes the reward is returning a lost item to its owner.

Shipwrecks have yielded many amazing jewelry finds, including necklaces, rings, and pins.

An emerald and gold cross salvaged in 1986 from the shipwreck Atocha, which sank in 1622.

XTREME QUOTE
"Today's the day!"
–Mel Fisher, Treasure Hunter
He said it every day for more than 16 years before finding the Atocha in 1985.

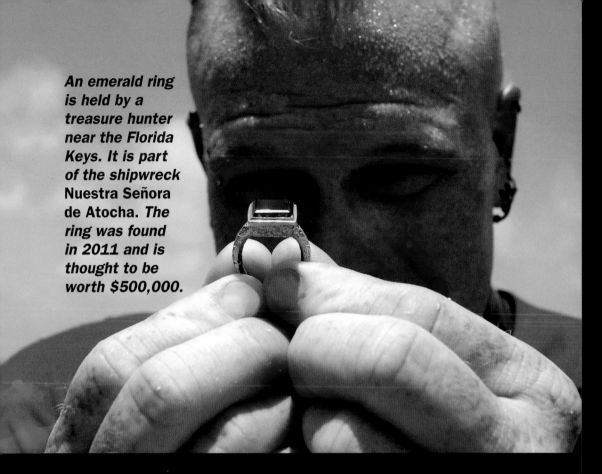

An emerald ring is held by a treasure hunter near the Florida Keys. It is part of the shipwreck Nuestra Señora de Atocha. *The ring was found in 2011 and is thought to be worth $500,000.*

An emerald brooch (pin) from the Nuestra Señora de las Maravillas. *The Spanish ship sank in 1656 off Grand Bahama Island, about 56 miles (90 km) off the state of Florida. While items have been found, the wreck area is still being searched today.*

HUNTING FOR SILVER

Silver was commonly transported in ships. It is very valuable. Silver coins, ingots, and bars have been discovered in several shipwrecks. The SS *Gairsoppa*, a merchant ship sunk during World War II off the coast of Ireland, yielded 1,203 bars of silver valued at about $38 million.

Treasure hunters bring up silver bars from the SS Gairsoppa.

The Spanish ship *La Capitana* struck a reef and sank in 1654. It carried tons of silver ingots and coins. Much of it was salvaged right after it sank. However, not all the silver was recovered. Using the diary of a survivor, treasure hunters rediscovered *La Capitana* off the coast of Ecuador in 1996. They salvaged nearly 4,000 silver coins, two silver ingots, and other artifacts valued at nearly $400 million.

HUNTING FOR GOLD

Finding gold is a treasure hunter's dream come true. Gold coins, bars, and jewelry are sometimes found in shipwrecks.

Treasure hunter David Booth is shown with the 2,000-year-old gold neck "torcs" he discovered with his metal detector.

Some metal detectors can be programmed to find gold. Many treasure hunters look for gold objects in the ground. Others use their metal detectors to search for the raw metal. Once a positive hit occurs, treasure hunters pan for gold flakes and nuggets. It's hard work, but some people find riches.

A rich payoff of gold flakes and nuggets from a treasure hunt.

Treasure hunters pan for gold.

HUNTING FOR GLASS & BOTTLES

Glass containers that once held medicines, snuff, ink, alcohol, milk, fruits, or vegetables are valuable treasure. Antique bottles and ceramic jugs are often found in abandoned dumps, outhouses, or yards. These items are pieces of history and are treasured by collectors.

A treasure hunter digs in an old outhouse hole.

A glass bottle for Warner's Safe Kidney & Liver Cure and a ceramic jug are among the finds from an outhouse dig. These items may be worth $25-250 each.

HUNTING FOR ARTIFACTS

Artifacts are anything of a historical nature, such as arrowheads, pottery, or medals. Treasure hunters search areas where ancient people lived or where battles were fought. Archaeologists, scientists, and historians with special training may be employed to properly excavate an important find. Museums are often the purchasers of these treasured relics.

Some call treasure hunting for artifacts "land fishing."

An Ohio treasure hunter has found such artifacts as keys, a perfume bottle, silverware, and a deputy marshal badge.

A collection of metal and clay artifacts found in a Spanish shipwreck.

WHERE TO HUNT

Luck, persistence, and research can lead to discovering treasure. People of all ages have found great historical treasures. Most beaches and parks are public property and are good places to hunt. State and national parks and forests have rules against disturbing potential archaeological finds. It is important to find out a park's specific rules before treasure hunting.

To search on private property, treasure hunters must get permission from the landowner. Whatever is found is the landowner's property. However, most treasure hunters and landowners make an agreement as to who gets what percentage of a find BEFORE anything is even searched for. Treasure hunting can be profitable, but above all, it is an adventure.

GLOSSARY

ARCHAEOLOGIST
A person who searches for, uncovers, and studies artifacts from the past in order to learn how people of ancient societies once lived.

ARTIFACTS
Objects made or owned by a person or group of people. Often of historical interest, artifacts can be something worn, like clothing or jewelry, or something used, such as dishes or tools, or something created by a culture, such as art.

CAST COINS
Coins made by pouring melted metal into a mold.

GPS (GLOBAL POSITIONING SYSTEM)
A system of orbiting satellites that transmits information to GPS receivers on Earth. Using information from the satellites, receivers can calculate location, speed, and direction with great accuracy.

HAMMERED COIN
A coin made by placing a metal disk (usually gold or silver) between two shaped dies (often wooden) and striking the top die with a hammer. Hammered coins were used in Europe, the Middle East, and the New World between about 600 AD to 1700 AD.

Ingot

A block of metal made by melting a metal, such as silver or gold, and pouring it into a mold to produce a specific weight and size that is easily stored.

Milled Coin

A coin made by a machine known as a mill. The edges of the coin are often raised or have vertical grooves.

Salvage

Recovering lost cargo and other items, such as from a shipwreck.

Snuff

Powered tobacco that is sniffed up a person's nostril.

Torc

A band of twisted metal that is worn around the neck.

World War II

A war that was fought from 1939 to 1945, involving countries around the world.

INDEX